Christina Aguilera

An Unauthorized Biography

BY JACKIE ROBB

A HarperEntertainment Book
from HarperPerennial

For my mom, Olga

Also by Jackie Robb

Britney Spears: The Unauthorized Biography

FIRST EDITION
Designed by Jeanette Jacobs
Library of Congress Cataloguing-in-Publication data is available on file.
Visit HarperEntertainment on the World Wide Web at http://www.harpercollins.com

99 00 01 02 03 10 9 8 7 6 5 4 3 2 1

Contents

She's talented, trendy, smart, and majorly cool—she's 18-year-old Christina Aguilera, and she's the latest in a line of pop princesses destined to take over the world—or at least the music world!

Introduction

Like her friend Britney Spears (from their days as Mouseketeers on the *Mickey Mouse Club*), Christina is everywhere—on MTV, appearing on TV shows like *Beverly Hills, 90210*, and, especially, on the radio, where her first single, "Genie in a Bottle," soared to the number one position in just a few short weeks.

The Club!

Christina made her early show business mark when she appeared on the Disney Channel show the *Mickey Mouse Club*. She was twelve when she earned her ears, but she'd been entertaining people since she was a child. "That feeling I got when I was performing, it was incredible," Christina told *16* magazine. "I never forgot it. I always wanted that feeling to be with me. And performing was the way to get it!"

The Magic Touch!

Before 1999, fans of Christina followed her rise to fame first as a Mouseketeer, then as a movie soundtrack singer in the movie *Mulan*. It was Christina's magnificent voice you heard when the poignant ballad "Reflection" played as the credits rolled. But what you probably didn't know is this—the same week Christina was recording "Reflection," she was also offered a record deal with RCA Records (the same record company that signed on 'N Sync, the boy group that includes Justin Timberlake and J. C. Chasez, two more of Christina's friends from the *Mickey Mouse Club*.) Coincidence? Who knows?

But Christina set out to show that she was far from a one-hit wonder. She proved she had the real golden touch again when she released her first single, the catchy "Genie in a Bottle." Before you knew it, that gets-in-your-head-and-you-can't-get-it-out song with the hummable chorus, "I'm a genie in a bottle, baby / Gotta rub me the right way, honey," was being sung by everyone under the sun.

Hitting the Road

It wasn't long before Christina started doing concerts and public appearances all across the planet. She was a huge hit in Japan; she totally sparkled in Europe; and she rocked the house down in the U.S. Audiences everywhere were able to identify with her emotional, powerful songs—lyrics that talked about love, life, growing up, and the struggle to find one's own identity.

But Christina's hardly struggling now. In fact, she's having a pretty easy time fitting into her new identity: that of pop superstar—her years of professional training on the *Mickey Mouse Club*

combined with her awesome natural abilities make her an inspiring, vibrant stage personality. From the moment she steps onto the stage and under those bright lights, Christina's really got the power.

Christina Power!

And Christina is more than just an amazing singer—she's also a talented actress who's already been approached by various directors for roles in TV and films. Of course, that's not surprising—those years on the *Mickey Mouse Club* prepared Christina for absolutely anything! (The show challenged its young stars to flex their performance muscles. They had to sing, dance, and even act in skits!)

Keepin' It Real!

But in addition to being a multi-talented performer, Christina is an all-around nice girl—the kind of person you'd really like to get to know. She has a big family that keeps her grounded and centered and enables her to experience things typical teens do. Like most kids her age, she still enjoys the fun, everyday things in life—shopping, chatting on the phone with close friends, and spending time with the ones she loves. But she also has a determined, hardworking, and ambitious side. Christina loves what she does and she always gives 100 percent to her work. And hard work it is! It's not easy scoring a number one song, a hot first album, or an appearance on MTV. Christina's always dreamed of success in the music business, and her life's goal was to perform and make others happy—but it definitely took a lot of work to get there!

So who exactly is Christina Aguilera, and how did she capture the hearts of so many fans, male and female? How did she get her start? What does her future hold? For the answers to these and many other questions, you gotta sit back, get comfortable, and enjoy the read.

Christina Maria Aguilera was born on December 18, 1980, in Staten Island, New York. Her mom, Shelley, was a violinist and pianist who, as a teenager herself, had traveled all over Europe with the Youth Symphony Orchestra.

Beginnings

(When Christina was a teenager pursuing her own musical dreams, she often said, "I use my mom's performing experience against her sometimes. I say, 'If you did it, I can do it!'") Christina definitely inherited her mother's love of music, which always filled the house.

Christina's dad, Fausto (who was born in Ecuador), was in the military, and Christina's early years were spent traveling.

Traveling in the military means serious moving around, so by the time Christina was just eight years old, she had already lived in Japan, Florida, Texas, and New Jersey. The family finally settled in Wexford, Pennsylvania, a small suburb of Pittsburgh.

Shelley is of Irish descent, but she was training to become a Spanish translator when she met Fausto. Christina's parents split up when she was young—she prefers to keep private about that and about her dad in general. But the one thing she openly reminisces about is growing up listening to both her parents speaking Spanish.

It wasn't long before Shelley

realized that her blond, blue-eyed daughter had received the gift of musical talent. That kind of talent wasn't exactly hard to notice—especially when Christina would sing in the bathtub, using a bottle of shampoo as a microphone! "I guess I started singing when I was about five or six," Christina told 16 magazine. "Kids would come over and ask if I could come out and play, and my mom would say I was playing—singing by myself. I guess some people might have thought I was weird."

But Shelley didn't think her talented daughter was weird at all, and when Christina started expressing an interest in performing, her mom encouraged her to go for it. Soon, Christina was a staple at local block parties and talent shows singing songs from her favorite Rodgers and Hammerstein musical, *The Sound of Music*.

Jude Pohl, the director of Pittsburgh Theater Company/Pohl Productions, remembers the competitive kid who never failed to wow audiences and judges alike. "She was a little girl with an adult voice," he told the *Pittsburgh Post-Gazette*. "She was always the undefeated champion in talent shows."

After winning these local con-tests, there was nowhere to go but up, up, and away. She took her powerful pipes to the whole coun-try—to the well-known talent show *Star Search*. She was eight when she tried out for the show at an open audition in Pittsburgh, and nine when she appeared on the nationally televised show. She didn't win—and she admits that she cried ner-vously backstage—but she still made a glori-ous impression.

Although she returned to Wexford without a *Star Search* trophy, she did have a touch of local fame, and it wasn't long before the "big boys" came calling—the big boys who play professional football and hockey that is! Christina was invited to sing the national anthem for the Pittsburgh Steelers and the Pittsburgh Penguins.

It was all pretty intense for a shy, introverted girl who preferred playing in her room to socializing with friends. But there was something about performing—about getting in front of an audience and just singing, that brought Christina tremendous joy, and she just knew she had to continue doing it. "I never just decided to be a singer," she told the *Pittsburgh Post-Gazette.* "It was always a dream for me. My love of it just carried me along."

Although Christina continued to appear at local events in Wexford, there just weren't enough opportunities for her to perform as much as she wanted to. She dreamed of going further, of singing in front of even larger crowds, and of showing the world exactly what she could do. She went to school, hung out with friends, and did all the things young people do—but she knew she wanted more.

Then one day, her mom read about another open audition in Pittsburgh, this one for a well-known, nationally televised variety show called the *Mickey Mouse Club.* Shelley and Christina drove to the audition, and although she was nervous, she gave it her best shot. The producers were impressed with her ability, her stage presence, and her obvious talent, but they were concerned about her young age—she was only ten, and most of the Mouseketeers were already teenagers.

It would be two long years before Shelley got the call—could she bring Christina down to Orlando, where the *Mickey Mouse Club* was filmed? The producers of the show had recognized Christina's awesome abilities and they couldn't wait any longer—they wanted her to join the *Club!*

Christina couldn't have been more excited to join up with the gang at the MICKEY MOUSE CLUB.

Makin' it Happen at the Mouse Club

At the age of twelve, she was one of the Club's younger members—the same age as a very adorable, curly-haired young boy named Justin Timberlake, and one year older than a sweet-voiced girl named Britney Spears.

By the time Christina became a full-fledged Mouseketeer (as the *Club* members were called), the show was entering its sixth season and was one of the Disney Channel's top-rated shows. It was filmed in front of a live audience at Walt Disney World's MGM Studios, so Christina got to entertain people face-to-face—live!

This incarnation of the show first appeared on the air in 1988, and its concept was simple and entertaining. The producers brought together young people between the ages of eleven and nineteen and created a true variety show. The Mouseketeers would sing, dance, act in comedy skits, and interact with celebrity guest stars. The show's fun side was complemented by a more serious, socially conscious side. Each episode focused on issues that were important to teens, from drugs and peer pressure, to school and family problems.

Ear Power!

Christina, Britney, and Justin—along with fellow newcomers Nikki DeLoach, Ryan Gosling, Tate Lynche, and T. J. Fantini—debuted on *MMC* in the fall of 1993.

Christina moved to Orlando with her mom, and they shared an apartment near the studio where the show was taped each day. "It was so cool, going to work at Disney World," Christina told *Tiger Beat* magazine. "It was such fun, being a part of the show, and being in Orlando. And working with such wonderful people—we were just like brothers and sisters!"

Christina immediately became a very popular *Club* member. Her impressive voice, her dynamic stage presence, and her sparkling personality made her a favorite with fans around the country. She began receiving fan mail and popping up in a variety of magazines for younger readers. Fans learned that her nickname (back then) was Funky Diva or Mariah, that she adored steak-and-potato dinners, and that she considered her worst quality to be her lack of patience. She was quoted as saying, "The roughest road is often the one that leads straight to the top." She urged her fans to "make good goals, and work to reach them" because "anything is possible with hard work and determination."

Although Christina was young, she was no rookie performer—she'd always known she could sing, and this gave her confidence in front of the live audience she performed for every week. All the

traveling she'd done growing up gave her added maturity. And she had a strong work ethic—she loved everything about her job, from the rehearsal to the final performance.

Well, almost everything! She was not particularly fond of one comedy skit she did with her fellow Mouseketeers. "I had to have a pie thrown in my face," she told *Teen People* magazine. "That wasn't too fun." Still, she got through the skit like a trouper. At a young age, Christina was already a pro, happy to learn and eager to show off her skills.

Life as a Mouseketeer wasn't always easy. The *Club* team worked from Tuesday through Saturday, so Christina had to be up at 7:00 each morning to catch the van that took her and her *MMC* buds to a special school on the show's back lot. They were tutored from 9 A.M. to 12:30 P.M. (Christina loved science and English best. She wasn't a huge fan of math.) After school came rehearsals, which ran from one to three hours; hair, wardrobe, and makeup followed, and by 3:45, Christina was ready to go on. The show would be taped for three hours, after which Christina would head home to eat dinner and do her homework. It was tough, but she loved it. "I learned so much there," she told *All-Stars* magazine.

Christina didn't mind the grueling work schedule—in fact, she enjoyed being a part of the enthusiastic and exciting process of putting on a variety show. But she says that what made the show even more memorable were the strong friendships she made among her fellow Mouseketeers—most notably, young Britney Spears; the two became really close buds. "We were all so close," Christina told *Teen Beat* magazine. "Maybe it was

because we were together all the time, but we just bonded so quickly and so strongly."

For Christina, her time at the *Mickey Mouse Club* gave her two important gifts. The first was the experience of a lifetime—the chance to work on her singing, dancing, and acting; the chance to perform for wildly appreciative audiences. The second was that she proved to herself that she wanted and loved to perform— that singing onstage was the life she wanted for herself. "It was a wonderful education for me," she told the *Los Angeles Times*. "Being on the show gave me so much confidence in myself. It taught me so much about discipline and hard work—the lessons I would need if I was really going to succeed in the music business."

Christina had spent two years on the *Mickey Mouse Club* when the show was abruptly canceled (to the sadness of hundreds of thousands of fans, who still bombard the Disney Channel with letters and E-mail asking them to bring it back). She was incredibly disappointed, but more ambitious and determined than ever—she knew now what her future could hold, and she was ready to chase her dreams and her goals. But before she could reflect on her life for long, she was on the road again!

Christina's MMC Stats!

Although Christina had been dreaming of fame in the music business forever, she wasn't prepared for the interest her fans immediately took in her—and *Mickey Mouse Club* fans wanted to know absolutely everything about the little girl with the majorly huge voice. Teen magazines were always busy interviewing the cast of *MMC*, and Christina was no exception to that rule.

Back in 1993, when Christina first joined the *MMC* team, she filled out a fact sheet that listed her favorite things—here's what she wrote when she was just thirteen years old!

1. **Color:** Turquoise and purple
2. **TV Show:** *Step by Step*
3. **Movie:** *Big*
4. **Actors:** Tom Hanks and Julia Roberts
5. **Singers:** Whitney Houston, En Vogue, Boyz II Men
6. **Song:** "I Will Always Love You," by Whitney Houston
7. **Food:** Steak, potatoes, and pizza
8. **Ice Cream Flavor:** Strawberry, chocolate
9. **Book:** *The Time of the Witch*
10. **Vacation Spot:** California
11. **Sport:** Hockey
12. **Sports Team:** Pittsburgh Penguins
13. **School Subject:** English and science
14. **Hobbies:** Dancing, sports, singing, and acting
15. **Best Day of Her Life:** "When I was picked to be a Mouseketeer on the show!"

The MICKEY MOUSE CLUB Hall of Fame!

The *MMC* Mouseketeers were no ordinary group of young performers— they were extraordinarily talented teenagers who sang, danced, and acted in comedy skits each and every week. And from this group of amazing artist came an astonishing number of actors and pop singers currently making news on TV, in the movies, on the radio, and on concert stages across the country. Check them out!

Keri Russell: She was one of the "big kids," according to Christina—Keri was already a poised, polished performer; a young lady with rare grace and talent. The curly-haired golden

9

girl who always had a smile on her face seemed destined for superstardom even then. She appeared in the 1996 NBC drama *Malibu Shores* before riding the fame-wave with the title role on the smash hit show *Felicity*. In 1998, Keri won a Golden Globe Award for Best Performance by an Actress in a Dramatic TV Series. According to Christina, everyone totally idolized Keri. "She was so cool—she was the first one to fray her jeans, which was so cool at the time," Christina told *YM* magazine. "And she was so beautiful—we were all in awe of her."

Tony Lucca: This other "big kid" found more than fame on *MMC*, he found love—he and Keri Russell have been a loving couple since their days on the *Mickey Mouse Club* (they started dating when they were very young). These days, Tony is pursuing his love of music—he's a songwriter, singer, and musician

whose CD can be purchased over the Internet. The two live in California.

J. C. Chasez and Justin Timberlake: Oh, those adorable 'N Sync guys! Justin and J. C. stayed tight after the cancellation of the *Mickey Mouse Club*, and both continued to take voice lessons and work on their dancing techniques. In 1997, when pop music was heating up the charts again, the determined pair teamed up with Chris Kirkpatrick, Joey Fatone, and Lance Bass—and the rest is 'N Sync history! Both guys remember their *Mickey Mouse Club* days with pride. "You were given so much freedom on that show," Justin recalls. "You were never restricted to one type of music. You got to dip your fingers into everything. It was the best preparation I could hope for. It taught us all how to be spontaneous—if anything goes wrong onstage, I can roll with it because of my experiences on *MMC*."

Britney Spears: One of Christina's best *MMC* friends was pop princess Britney Spears—the two were very close in age and had a lot in common. These days, of course, Britney is enjoying life in the pop lane—her debut album, *. . . Baby One More Time*, was a monster number one hit, as were the top-selling singles ". . . Baby One More Time," "Sometimes," and "Crazy." Britney remembers the *Mickey Mouse Club* with total fondness, and she giggles when she thinks about her good times with Christina. "We were the babies," she told *16* magazine. "We were treated extra-special, because we were so young. It was a lot of fun."

Other Club Members

Nikki Deloach: This Southern singing sensation is currently working with the pop girl group Innosense. "Nikki is probably the next breakout star from *Mickey Mouse Club*," Christina told *Tiger Beat* magazine. "She's a great talent."

Ryan Gosling: The young actor with the mischievous smile starred in the TV show *Young Hercules*, which filmed in New Zealand.

Josh Ackerman: The sarcastic, adorable comedian of the *Club*, Josh is currently working on his first love, music.

Rhona Bennett: The gal who wowed audiences with her awesome voice is currently working on her debut album.

The *Mickey Mouse Club* was much more than a fun, wacky weekly comedy/variety show—it was actually an amazing breeding ground for some of the most talented young people to rock the American entertainment world in a long time. But according to Christina, all these astounding, gifted people were just good buds back then. "We used to joke around backstage and say, 'Whenever the show ends, we'll all go off our separate ways and become stars,'" Christina told *USA Today*. "We were all so determined and driven—I'm not surprised at any of the success of my co-Mouseketeers."

Christina is also psyched that lots of her fans from those *MMC* days are still with her, supporting her. "I had so many fans that followed me from *Mickey Mouse Club*," she told *Superteen* magazine. "Fans will come up to me and tell me how much they love my music—and then they'll say how much they loved *Mickey Mouse Club*. It's a great feeling, to have such supportive fans in my life."

Departing from the fun, excitement, and constant activity of the MICKEY MOUSE CLUB left Christina feeling slightly out of sorts.

MULAN

She returned home to Wexford, Pennsylvania, but she knew she wouldn't be satisfied hanging out in her room. She also found that she and her old schoolmates and friends had really grown apart over the years Christina was away. "A lot of my classmates ignored me," Christina told the *Los Angeles Times*. "I guess I was a bit of an outcast, since I was working on a TV show and basically away from school for so long." And that wasn't the worst of it—jealous classmates even went so far as to slash the tires on her mom's car!

Christina knew she couldn't continue to go to public school and pursue her musical dreams at the same time, so she continued her education with a tutor. Being taught this way gave Christina the chance to work—whenever that chance came!

As it turned out, Christina was destined to be back in the spotlight sooner than even she expected. It wasn't long before she was actually looking back on those memories and feelings of isolation—and using them to fuel her singing voice with emotion!

To a World Far Away!

While Christina was working on the *Mickey Mouse Club*, she caught the attention of Steve Kurtz, who asked to become her manager. He urged Christina to record a demo tape, which he sent to RCA Records Artists & Repertoire Director Ron Fair.

Christina was still working hard to pursue her musical dreams—this time on another con-

12

tinent. Her *Mickey Mouse Club* fame was still sizzling in Japan, so she traveled there and recorded a duet called "All I Wanna Do" with Japanese pop star Keizo Nakanishi. She appeared in the music video that accompanied the song, and she toured the country as well. Later that same year, she traveled to Transylvania, Romania, to perform at the Golden Stag Festival, and a near-riot broke out when she sang two songs—the crowd couldn't get enough of her, even though superstars Sheryl Crow and Diana Ross were waiting in the wings to take the stage.

Fast-Forward to . . . MULAN!

Christina again returned to her hometown, and waited. She continued being tutored and pursuing her usual hobbies—shopping and playing sports. But this time she had a feeling that something was about to happen—something big.

Meanwhile, over at RCA Records, A&R director Ron Fair got a call from Christina's old employers, the folks at Disney. Seems they were getting ready to make a new animated film called *Mulan*, and they were looking for a young girl who could really belt out—an especially hard musical note, high E-flat above middle C. Ron remembered the powerful voice he'd heard on Christina's demo tape and he immediately called her with the opportunity of a lifetime.

Christina knew she could do it—and she was more than willing to prove it. She grabbed her tape recorder, sang the notes they wanted to hear, and sent the tape to Ron. A few days later, Christina was flown to the Disney Studios in Los Angeles, and handed a lovely song called "Reflection." She sang it for them several times—the Disney executives listening in were awed by the power in her voice and the emotion in her delivery. She got the job right then and there.

Christina went to work in the recording studio, and for one week, she sang "Reflection" over and over again. "You mess things up, things happen, and you have to start over," Christina told the *Pittsburgh Post-Gazette*. "It was no big deal—every singer has to deal with it."

After the recording session ended, Christina planned to fly home, but first she stayed around to hear a ninety-piece orchestra accompany her voice on the recorded song. "It was enough to bring tears to my eyes," she said. "It was so amazing to hear that beautiful music."

The Story of MULAN

Walt Disney's thirty-sixth animated film, *Mulan*, was destined for greatness from the moment it was released. It is a tale of one girl's journey in a story of true heroism, self-discovery, and triumph that fans of all ages could relate to.

Mulan tells of a free-spirited young girl who doesn't exactly fit into the traditional, conservative Chinese society she was born to. She discovers that her elderly father has been ordered to help defend China against the invading Huns. To protect him from a situation that would surely cause his death, she bravely disguises herself as a man so that she can take her father's place in the Imperial Army.

Mulan arrives at the army camp to be trained by the handsome Captain Shang. She is aided in her brave quest by her guardian dragon, Mushu, and her lucky cricket, Cri-Kee. Mulan blossoms into a skilled soldier who brings victory to the nation by defeating the ruthless and evil leader of the Huns, Shan-Yu. Mulan's bravery brings honor to her family name, and she also finds true love.

Reflections on "Reflection"

Christina breathed life into the song "Reflection." She interpreted the lyrics, which talk about believing in yourself and finding your place in the world, simply by using her voice. And she completely identified with Mulan, who needed to find a way to fit into her world, and who was seeking her own self-identity—after all, hadn't Christina experienced the same things?

The film *Mulan* was a huge success, and when the credits rolled, it was Christina's voice the world heard singing the pop version of "Reflection." "I was ecstatic," she told the *Providence Journal*. "They took a huge chance using an unknown like me. These kinds of things only happen once every few years."

The song "Reflection" was nominated for a Golden Globe Award in 1998. It also rose to number 15 on the Adult/Contemporary music charts. But for Christina, the reward was something much more personal. For the very same week that Christina was recording "Reflection," she heard the fabulous news—RCA Records had signed her to a record deal of her very own. The little girl looking for a place to fit in had finally found one.

Christina got the news while she was busy recording "Reflection"—she'd been signed to a record deal with RCA Records (the same company, by the way, that signed another incredibly hot pop act, 'N Sync).

For the Record

As soon as *Mulan*-mania began to die down, Christina found herself back in the studio, recording her very own album. The record company brought in only the best producers and songwriters in the business to create the glorious music Christina would sing.

RCA's A&R director, Ron Fair, was delighted with his new young singer and full of confidence for her success. "Christina is absolutely fearless," he told the *Los Angeles Times*. "I was struck by her amazing voice, her budding beauty, and I decided to take a shot and sign her."

Christina was seventeen when she started working on the album, and she was psyched that she was about to fulfill one of her greatest goals. "I always dreamed of recording an album before I finished high school," she bubbled to the *Los Angeles Times*. "And now I'm actually doing it!"

On the Road Already!

In addition to recording the album, Christina was also busy traveling. RCA Records took Christina out on an artist's showcase—an arena where people in the music business get an early listen to talent with potential. This time they got to hear an

amazing pop diva-to-be in action. She visited New York City, Los Angeles, Toronto, Canada, Las Vegas, and Minneapolis, and performed for industry bigwigs with only a piano to back her up. The word was out—this was a singer to watch—closely!

Christina was totally floored by the praise. She was also thrilled to have the chance to visit so many new places. "I really like the traveling part of this business," she told *Teen Beat* magazine. "I wish I had more time to really sightsee, but just being in a new city is exciting. I don't think I'll ever get tired of it."

The Album Takes Shape—and a "Genie" Takes Center Stage!

As Christina recorded her album, she was happy to hear it taking a very danceable turn—anyone who expected the whole CD to sound just like "Reflection"

would be very surprised indeed. Christina's influences were mostly rhythm and blues–based—artists like Mariah Carey and Whitney Houston had been able to blend R&B and pop music successfully, and so would Christina!

The songs on the album were also headed in a very mature, more grown-up direction. Christina's voice was big and strong enough to handle the most powerful ballads, but she also had the talent to convey a whole wide range of emotions. This would be an album that young kids, teenagers, and their parents would all be able to listen and dance to.

When the recording process was over, everyone sat back and listened to what Christina had accomplished. There was no doubt it was going to be huge, but there was one major decision that had to be made. What would be the first single? What song would act as Christina's reintroduction to the musical world—and the rest of the world as well? The record company execs knew they needed to choose a song that had a little magic going for it—and there would be no doubt that that song was "Genie in a Bottle."

Christina's first single, "Genie in a Bottle," was released to radio stations on June 22, 1999. It didn't take long for Christina—and the world—to know she had a bona fide hit on her hands.

Genie Uncorked

Almost over night, the whole world was singing along to the hypnotic chorus and the cool, catchy lyrics.

In only a month the single flew to number one on the music charts—number one throughout the United States! And the only person who was really surprised about the song's success was Christina herself.

Christina actually had some misgivings about recording "Genie in a Bottle," even though she recognized that it was very commercial and radio-friendly. She was concerned about the song's lyrics, which she thought might be misconstrued by listeners. "At first, I was a little afraid that some people might not completely get where I'm coming from in the song," she told *Billboard* magazine.

"It's about self-respect. It's about not giving in to temptation until you're respected."

The Songwriter Speaks!

Every songwriter in the world dreams of having his or her tune recorded by an awesome singer, and Steve Kipner, who cowrote "Genie in a Bottle," is no exception. He was psyched to hear his words sung by Christina, and he was totally floored by her powerful voice and remarkable talent. "She had abilities you usually only see in older, more experienced artists," he told the *Los Angeles Times*. "She used lessons she'd learned from artists like Mariah Carey and Chaka Khan, and created her own, amazing sound. She's just extraordinary." Steve and Christina agree that the song's catchiest moment, the little "Come, come, come on in" hook, was actually created by Christina herself. "That was my whole writing thing on 'Genie,'" she joked to *Tiger Beat* magazine. "But I definitely want to write more in the future. And I want to produce music for other artists—gosh, wouldn't it be amazing to work with Mariah? I'd love to do a duet with her!"

A Picture's Worth a Thousand Words!

Meanwhile, the video for "Genie in a Bottle" was released to MTV and The Box, and, of course, it was a screaming success. It quickly became one of the top four most requested videos, becoming what MTV's *Total Request Live* calls "buzzworthy."

Directed by Diane Martel, the video highlights Christina's sultry, elegant vocal style while providing a seriously watchable video story. In it, Christina's "genie" is discovered by a waiting and willing "master." But she musically informs him that she's not some *I Dream Of Jeannie* fantasy—she's not coming out of her bottle until he promises to treat her with respect, until he promises to make her wishes come true. In powerful close-ups, Christina's bright blue-green eyes tell the viewer that she's aware of the power of her magic—and she

doesn't plan to waste it, or her love, on just any scrub guy.

The video was immediately added into MTV's heavy rotation, and became a huge fan favorite. MTV's senior programmer Tom Calderone praised Christina's "amazing star quality."

Of course, everyone could see that the cameras totally loved Christina. There was something about her expressive eyes and her sweet, soulful expression that made hundreds of thousands of young fans identify with her. In one four-minute video Christina fully connected with her audience—and her audience totally fell in love with her.

Taking the Next Step!

With the release of one awesome single, Christina saw one of her dreams come true: her vocal ability—her pure, clear, powerful singing—voice and amazing power to intuitively understand and interpret a song had brought her total fame. All the attention might have blown away someone less grounded, modest, and sure of herself, but Christina remained

sweet and humble. And despite the buzz that surrounded her every move, Christina also remained shy and introspective, never getting herself caught up in the hype generated by the press and the constant photographers snapping her picture. She did, however, look forward to meeting her fans—the ones who made her face famous on the Internet, the ones who sang along when "Genie in a Bottle" played on the radio. "I can't wait for the day fans recognize me on the street," she told the *Los Angeles Times*. "I know some people hate that, but not me. I've been waiting for this moment all my life."

Golden Girl

It wasn't long before Christina brought home the gold—as in a gold record! "Genie in a Bottle" quickly sold over a million copies, and became the monster radio hit of the summer of '99. But Christina was already thinking about her debut album—the one she'd spent so much time working on. It had been over a year since she first stepped into the recording the studio, and she knew the time was right—the "genie" had done its magic, and now it was time for the rest of the album to sizzle through the remaining dog days of summer. Christina was thinking about what the fan reaction would be

when the world heard all of her music. She knew her album would represent a risk—so much of the music on it was different from the pop sound of "Genie in a Bottle"; so much of it was a celebration of the rhythm and blues music Christina had loved all her life. And most of all, she hoped her music could make a difference; could really touch the people who heard it. "I really want to make music that makes kids feel confident and secure," she told *Billboard* magazine. "I'm looking forward to reaching out and touching as many fans as possible. It's really time for something different."

And that "something different" was on its way. Christina Aguilera was going to have her say, on the debut album that would bear her name.

Christina's self-titled first album hit record stores on August 24, 1999, and from the second it came out of the box, the entire country was dancing to her tunes.

Christina:
The Album Says It All!

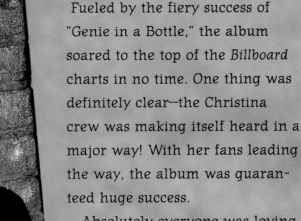

Fueled by the fiery success of "Genie in a Bottle," the album soared to the top of the *Billboard* charts in no time. One thing was definitely clear—the Christina crew was making itself heard in a major way! With her fans leading the way, the album was guaranteed huge success.

Absolutely everyone was loving Christina and the intense, sultry music she made. *Mademoiselle* magazine announced, "Move over Mariah Carey!" The magazine praised Christina's "rich voice," which they said had "range, maturity, and sensuality" that Christina used "with true diva aplomb."

The always modest, always humble young superstar-to-be was thoroughly gracious about the album's success, thanking the behind-the-scenes folks who worked hard to make it the best album it could be. "I was thrilled to work with so many great producers on the album," she gushed to *16* magazine.

Christina was justifiably proud of the work she had done on her debut CD. She was delighted with the spine-tingling ballads as well as the finger-snapping, toe-tapping, upbeat numbers. And her fans—now legions of them—were psyched to give the CD a spin. "I just hope everyone likes the record," she told *Teen Beat* magazine. "It means a lot to me to please the fans."

The producers turned to some of the most influential, popular and time-tested songwriters in the music business to pen the tunes that Christina would bring to life on her album. No expense was spared—some of the biggest chart-busting hit makers were brought in to write the songs Ms. Christina would sing to the world. Diane Warren, who's written such monster hits as "I Don't Want to Miss a Thing" from the smash-hit film *Armageddon*, contributed the spine-tingling ballad "I Turn to You." Travon Potts, who cowrote Monica's huge hit single "Angel of Mine," penned the tender, heartfelt single "Blessed." Christina was touched and honored to work with so many famous names, and thrilled to be in the company of such talented, creative people.

And they were thrilled to be working with her. Songwriter Diane Warren reported, "Christina is just the greatest singer. When she hits those high notes, you can really feel her talent." And writer/producer Steve Kipner was blown away the first time Christina sang "Genie in a Bottle" for him. "She owned that song," says Steve. "She took it and made it her own, her true signature song."

In the future, Christina would love to write some songs of her own, but these days she's concentrating on singing the songs, not penning them. "Sometimes I hear a song, and it's like it came straight out of my heart, even though someone else wrote it," Christina told *Teen Beat* magazine. "It's amazing how a truly great songwriter can touch anyone in the world with their words."

Christina Aguilera Makes the Grade!

There's no doubt that Christina's elegant, wistful, intense and magical voice speaks to a generation. Her songs touch on subjects that are important to everyone—love, relationships, and heartbreak, of course, but also strength, independence, and individuality. There are touching ballads that can soothe a broken heart; there are R&B tunes that make you sway and sing along; and there are way uptempo party songs that will make you want to dance the night away.

Here's the "inside track" on Christina Aguilera—and our "making the grade" reviews of each mesmerizing, magical, majorly excellent song!

"She's our Streisand," Ron Fair from RCA said.

Barbra Streisand

One of the most versatile, talented performers in the world, Barbra Streisand began her amazing career in the theater during the '60s, when she wowed Broadway with her amazing performance as Fanny Brice in FUNNY GIRL (she later won an Oscar when she starred in the movie version). Barbra's voice is considered a fine instrument—it is clear, true, and haunting. She's also an amazing actress, who's given awesome performances in films like THE WAY WE WERE, THE PRINCE OF TIDES, WHAT'S UP, DOC?, and YENTL. Although her fans are legion, she is notoriously nervous about performing live—her upcoming millennium concert at the MGM Grand Hotel in Las Vegas is a rare exception. She is truly the voice of a generation—a beautiful, powerful woman who's had total control of her career since day one. It's little wonder Christina looks to Barbra as a role model and source of inspiration.

Track 1:

"Genie in a Bottle"

Written by: Steve Kipner, David Frank, and Pam Sheyne

Produced by: David Frank and Steve Kipner

Tempo:

Midtempo, swayable; definitely a song you want to sing along to.

What Christina Says:

"A genie is always being portrayed as a man's slave. Now it's, 'I'm not coming out of my bottle unless you please me the way I want to be pleased.' It's a total girl-power song."

What It's All About:

What she said! It also says any guy who lets her out of her bottle better be ready to make a good impression.

Grade: A+++

A very cool tune with smart, witty lyrics. And the catchiest chorus in town.

Track 2:

"What a Girl Wants"

Written by: Shelly Peiken and Guy Roche

Produced by: Guy Roche

Tempo:

Uptempo, with definite R&B flava.

What Christina Says:

"I think this song is really powerful—it makes it clear that there are certain things a girl really can't live without in a boyfriend."

What It's All About:

An appreciative girlfriend sings the praises of her very cool boyfriend, who's always there for her—which is just what every girl wants!

Grade: A+++

An excellent song with a chorus that makes you want to kick off your shoes, throw back your head, and sing at the top of your lungs!

Track 3:

"I Turn to You"

Written by: Diane Warren
Produced by: Guy Roche

Tempo:

It opens with the sound of pouring rain and thunder, than segues into a delicate, sweet ballad.

What Christina Says:

"Diane Warren really writes songs that touch your heart, and this is an example of that. This song really speaks to me."

What It's All About:

A young woman reveals to her love that he's her shelter from the storm, her friend, her strength, and her only one.

Grade: A+++

This ballad really exemplifies what Christina is all about. Her voice is so awesome it actually wraps around each word—the song positively soars. It's also a very powerful, loving song, and Christina really lets you know what she's feeling as she sings—it's like a living emotion.

Track 4:

"So Emotional"

Written by: Franne Golde and Tom Snow
Produced by: Ron Harris

Tempo:

R&B midtempo.

What Christina Says:

"I think everyone who's ever been in love can understand this song. It's really all about how people feel when they're in love—how their emotions just intensify, and really bubble up to the surface."

What It's All About:

A girl is spiritually, emotionally, and physically drawn to a mysterious love. She just can't help herself—her emotions are leading the way.

Grade: A++

This tune features some of Christina's richest vocal work—if you listen to this song, and concentrate on what she's doing with her voice, you know exactly what all the Christina-craziness is all about.

Track 5:
"Come on Over (All I Want Is You)"

Written by: Paul Rein and Johan Aberg

Produced by: Aaron Zigman, Paul Rein, and Johan Aberg

Tempo:

An excellent uptempo. This is the kind of song you would totally crank up if it played on your car radio and give your shocks a workout as you bop to the beat.

What Christina Says:

"This is such a fun song to sing. I think this one's really going to be a hit at concerts. It's got really good energy."

What It's All About:

A total good-time song. Our heroine tells her crush that he's the one for her—and urges him to spend some time with her to prove how perfect they'd be together.

Grade: A+++

Definitely one of the best songs on the album, "Come on Over" has an energy you'll get in to every time you hear it. The beat is strong—which will make you want to dance around your room—and the lyrics are smart, sassy, and real.

Track 6:
"Reflection"

Written by: Matthew Wilder and David Zippel (from the Disney Motion Picture *Mulan*)

Produced by: Matthew Wilder

Tempo:

A beautiful, introspective, and elegant ballad.

What Christina Says:

"The song's theme, the struggle to establish yourself and your identity, was something I could really relate to—especially since I'm a teenage girl myself, and I've gone through so much of those feelings."

What It's All About:

Mulan sings about the trials and sadness of hiding her true self beneath an elaborate costume—but rejoices in the knowledge that one day she'll reveal herself to the world. Listen closely—this is the song that gives Christina the chance to show off her awesome range.

Grade: A+++

This was the song that really got Christina noticed—and with good reason. It's stunning, powerful, positive, and filled with the pure emotion of a young person searching for her place in life. Like the title says, this song is muy "reflective"—it can really getting you thinking about the things going on in your own life.

Track 7:
"Love for All Seasons"

Written by: Carl Sturken and Evan Rogers

Produced by: Evan Rogers and Carl Sturken

Tempo:

Midtempo, with an R&B energy.

What Christina Says:

"A lot of people have told me that this song is very romantic, and I can certainly see why they would feel that way. I can imagine people in love singing it to one another."

What It's All About:

The singer promises the object of her affection that she'll be in his life every day of the year. No matter the weather—and no mat-

ter the difficulties they may face—her heart belongs to him.

Grade: A

Although this song doesn't have the most original theme, it's still powerful when it's being sung by a talent like Christina. She has a way of making words sound like pure poetry.

Track 8:
"Somebody's Somebody"

Written by: Diane Warren
Produced by: Khris Kellow

Tempo:

Swayable mid-tempo.

What It's All About:

Christina sings about her strong desire to be in a good relationship.

Grade: B

We know where you're coming from, Christina. Sometimes loneliness can tempt you to settle for any "somebody," "with two arms," "spending time with me." But deep down we know that only true love can fill an empty place in our lives. It's still a very cool song with lyrics lots of people can relate to—the dream of meeting someone special who'll be with you always. Just remember to be a little more discerning!

Track 9:

"When You Put Your Hands on Me"

Written by: Robin Thicke and J. Gass

Produced by: Robin Thicke and Pro "J"

Tempo:

Uptempo, a definite dance song.

What It's All About:

A girl is contemplating the amazing things that can happen when she's touched by the boy she loves.

Grade: A++

Looks like Christina's cornered the market on songs you can sway along to. This dance tune is powerful and intense—the best may keep you moving, but the lyrics will definitely strike a chord deep inside you.

Track 10:

"Blessed"

Written by: Travon Potts and Brock Walsh

Produced by: Travon Potts

Tempo:

Slow and serene, like a peaceful lake—a ballad of perfect beauty.

What Christina Says:

"I just love this song so much! It makes me grateful for all the wonderful things in my life."

What It's All About:

In this song, a young girl is thinking about all the blessings she's found in life—most particularly, the blessing of a most excellent love.

Grade: A+++

One of the most beautiful songs on the album, "Blessed" is one of those tunes you'll want to listen to again and again. It's also "blessed" with some of the most gorgeous backup vocals—the song sounds like a raindrop, if you can imagine that.

Track 11:

"Love Will Find a Way"

Written by: Carl Sturken and Evan Rogers

Produced by: Evan Rogers and Carl Sturken

Tempo:

A clap-along, uptempo tune that's bound to make you bounce your head and shoulders around.

What Christina Says:

"I'm really proud of my ballads, but I have to admit it's great to do these fun songs. I get such a good feeling when I sing it."

What It's All About:

A couple is experiencing some relationship ups and downs, but both know their love is worth fighting for—and they both know love will find a way to lead them through the tough times.

Grade: A+++

Another excellent song you're going to want to sing along to. Total, positive energy and enthusiasm.

Track 12:
"Obvious"

Written by: Heather Holley
Produced by: Robert Hoffman

Tempo:

A gentle, melodious ballad of depth and breathtaking beauty.

What Christina Says:

"This is another song I can totally identify with. It's about being afraid to show your feelings, being nervous about your 'obvious' emotions. I think everyone gets nervous to let others know what they're feeling."

What It's All About:

Our heroine is concerned that her emotions are too obvious to everyone around her. She's worried that her trembling hands and nervous stares are announcing her secret love to the world.

Grade: A+++

Elegant, lovely, simple, and real—hey, everybody's been where Christina is in this song! And as usual, Christina's powerful voice pushes the song to even greater heights.

To the outside world, it seemed like Christina was an overnight sensation—her debut CD rocked the world in what seemed like an instant.

The Genie Works Her Magic

But Christina and her family knew exactly how much hard work had gone into her success. They knew that it had taken years of determination and drive. They knew how she'd sacrificed, how she'd given up a lot of lazy weekends and fun times with friends to devote herself to her craft. And now she was more than ready to bask in the glow of success.

And that basking began almost immediately. Christina's self-titled CD debuted at number one on the Billboard charts! With "Genie in a Bottle" on everyone's radio, and Christina's album in practically every CD player on the planet, the world definitely could not get enough of her—everyone wanted to know absolutely everything about her. And they wanted to see her onstage.

The Choice of a Generation!

One of Christina's first live performances was on the 1999 Teen Choice Awards, sponsored by Fox-TV and *Seventeen* magazine. It was an awards show where the people got a chance to speak—ballots had been sent out across the country, and teenagers got the opportunity to voice in categories such as Choice Movie Actor and Actress, Best Hissy Fit and Sexiest Love Scene (in a big-screen movie), and Album of the Year. The guest list was enormous—artists like Britney Spears, 'N Sync, TLC, Aerosmith, and Gloria Estefan were scheduled to perform; Jennifer Love Hewitt, Melissa Joan Hart, Freddie Prinze, Jr., Sandra Bullock, and Jennifer Lopez sat in the audience.

Christina was psyched when she was asked to perform "Genie in a Bottle" (which had reached number one on the charts that very week) but she was also nervous. "This was the first time I ever performed that song live, with a band and dancers behind me," she told *Nickelodeon* magazine.

Of course, Christina's singing and dancing segment went off without a hitch. Dressed in a shimmery red top and dark blue jeans, Christina wowed the crowd with a picture-perfect performance. Although she wasn't an award winner that night, there was no doubt in anyone's mind that she would be, and soon.

TONIGHT, TONIGHT!

It didn't take long for Christina to become a sought-after guest on TV shows, but Christina—always modest, humble, and a little shy—took it all in stride. Most people might be quaking in their boots if they were told they were going to appear on *The Tonight Show* with host Jay Leno, but Christina only asked, "Which one is that?" She made her appearance on August 27, 1999, and as usual, she rocked the house down!

And of course, Christina is always a sought-after member of the pop music teen gang she appeared on *Summer Music Madness*, a concert special that aired on the UPN network, with her fellow former Mouseketeers Britney Spears, Justin Timberlake and J. C. Chasez (and the rest of 'N Sync), and popster Tyrese. "It's great to get together and work with other young people," she told *16* magazine. "It just goes to show, age has nothing to do with it—if you have a dream, and you work for it, it can be yours."

For the Fans!

Although Christina is now an artist in demand, she never, ever forgets the people who've brought her there. One of her favorite activities is jumping on the Internet to host and participate in online chats where she can really get to know her fans. "It's important to me to talk with my fans, and doing these chats is a great way to do that," she told *Billboard* magazine. "The questions they ask are always so intelligent, and I can really be myself with them."

Although Christina has little contact with and doesn't speak much about her dad, she's very proud of the heritage he passed down to her.

Salsa Roots

He was born in Ecuador, and perhaps because of that, Christina has a deep love of Latin and Spanish music.

These days, of course, the Latin music scene is positively jumping, and because of Christina's background, it was natural that her record company might consider having her join the Latin pack. But although Christina is proud of her Latino roots, she hasn't been linked to other Latin acts such as Ricky Martin, Jennifer Lopez, or Enrique Iglesias. According to Ron Fair, that's because RCA thinks Christina fits into more than one category musically. "She's of Latin descent, yes," he told the *Los Angeles Times*, "but I think she represents millions of kids across America who are of Hispanic descent, but are completely American. She's got the pipes to be the next Barbra Streisand or

Celine Dion, and to us, that's what really matters."

Still, Christina gets absolutely star-struck when she thinks about meeting Jennifer Lopez (whose music she adores). "I totally love Jennifer Lopez," she enthused to the *Los Angeles Times*. "I think what draws me to her is, I feel so proud of my Spanish roots, and the fact that she's Hispanic, and going out there and doing her thing. I can relate to that. Christina would also love to meet Enrique Iglesias (on whom she has a major crush)."

The Latin Line!

There's nothing hotter than the current wave of Latin music. Christina is a proud member of a distinguished group of performers who've brought the fierce, energetic, and invigorating beat of their heritage to the ears of an eager America audience. Here are just three of the many artists who are sizzling up the music charts in a very big way.

Ricky Martin

No one lives "la vida loca" like lovely Ricky Martin, who mesmerized audiences all over the country when he performed "La copa de la vida" at the 1999 Grammy Awards. He was born in "his" Puerto Rico on December 24, 1971, and started singing in grade school. Ricky got his first taste of international fame when he hooked up with the Latin boy group Menudo in 1984. After leaving the group in 1989, Ricky moved down to Mexico, where he became a regular on a Mexican soap opera called *Alcanzar una estrella II*. He released his first solo album in Spanish in 1992. It went gold in several countries.

Totally psyched by his solo success, Ricky moved to Los Angeles in 1994, and won a small role on the soap opera *General Hospital*. His third Spanish language album, *A medio vivir*, was a worldwide sensation. In the midst of this musical triumph, he won a role in the Broadway musical *Les Misérables*.

His fourth album, *Vuelve*, was already a planetwide hit when Ricky appeared on the Grammy Awards—and alerted the U.S. to what it had been missing! Ricky-

mania flourished, and his first English-language album, Ricky Martin, went straight to the top of the *Billboard* charts. Suddenly, Ricky was the man— everyone was singing his hot hit, "Livin' La Vida Loca," screaming at his concerts, and falling crazy in love with the Puerto Rican papi. With his sizzlin' sexiness and his awesome talent, Ricky is a true musical ambassador, who's brought a real salsa flavor to American pop.

Jennifer Lopez

Born in the Bronx, New York, on July 24, 1970, Jennifer Lopez dreamed of making it big. And she knew she had what it takes to do it all—that she could sing, dance, and act with the best of 'em. All she needed was a chance to totally prove it!

It took a ton of hard work, determination, and ambition (traits Christina most definitely shares with Jennifer, by the way) before Jennifer got her first taste of fame, appearing as a Fly Girl dancer on the TV show *In Living Color*. Even then, her special spark

35

and unbelievable energy caught everyone's eye.

Jennifer made her movie debut in 1995's *Money Train*, with Woody Harrelson. But it was her performance in the film *Selena*, which she starred in as the late Tejano singer, that really brought her attention. Audiences were surprised and psyched to hear that it was actually Jennifer singing those Selena tunes. Jennifer got her best critical reviews for the movie *Out of Sight*, in which she costarred with *ER*'s George Clooney.

Those who hadn't heard Jennifer sing in *Selena* were totally shocked to hear she was releasing an album—and even more surprised when they heard her awesome voice! Jennifer's album, *On the 6*, went platinum, as did her first single, "If You Had My Love," which went all the way to number one on the charts. There's no doubt Jennifer's the spiciest diva on the block!

Enrique Iglesias

It's little wonder that tall, dark, and handsome Enrique Iglesias floats Christina's boat—this romantic, sultry heartthrob has been making his female fans melt since he released his first album, *Enrique Iglesias*, in 1995. At 24, he's already an international sex symbol, just like his famous dad, Julio Iglesias, and his famous brother, Julio Iglesias, Jr.

With his latest album, *Bailamos*, Enrique has totally made his mark on the music world. The first single, "Bailamos," could be heard in the film *Wild Wild West*, starring Will Smith—talk about major exposure! And since then, he's been touring the world, bringing his special, sexy style of singing to fans who scream his name. There's no doubt that gorgeous Enrique is living his life's motto—"Live every day happy."

Clearly, the Latin music scene is exploding—and Christina will definitely be welcomed by her Latino following (she definitely intends to record an album in Spanish someday). But Christina also knows that truly great music transcends any categories—her stunning voice and emotional vocal style are sure to please everyone throughout the world in any language.

Christina was born on December 18, 1980, and that makes her a ragin' Sagittarius.

Christina's
Love Charts

Like many in her star sign, Christina obviously has diverse talents—she's a powerhouse singing talent, but she's also comfortable on stage and under the hot lights of the TV cameras. The music, movie, and theater world is filled with superstar Sagittarians, like Brad Pitt, Katie Holmes, Kim Basinger, and Brendan Fraser. Those born under the sign of the Archer tend to be straightforward and honest with a need to reach out and touch others in the world. Hmmm—maybe that's why lovely Christina is so good at reaching her thousands of fans with her magnificent voice and her sweet songs.

Other traits often associated with Sagittarians are friendliness and cheerfulness. Any fan who's had the opportunity to meet and chat with Christina knows those are two traits she absolutely radi-ates. That means when the chips are down, Christina remains upbeat and positive—she knows that a good attitude gives you the power to forge ahead, no matter what obstacles may stand in your way.

Of course, Sags also have another side—they can be overly ambitious, almost scarily driven to succeed. Christina doesn't deny she has that determined side—and she's been able to use it to help her build a fabulous career. And with all that ambition and energy, the future is totally open to her.

Those born under the sign of the Archer often say they feel lucky—Christina herself is often quoted as saying she feels like the luckiest person under the sun! But the truth is, it takes more than luck to build a successful music career, and Sagittarians know that, too! Those born under this sign enjoy taking chances and plunging into new things with lots of energy and enthusiasm—and these qualities probably have more to do with Christina's success than any "dumb luck." Christina's optimism and happy-go-lucky attitude, blended with the right amount of ambition, determination, and single-mindedness (and a heavy dose of hard work, don't forget!) have combined to bring her to this point in her career.

And that means whatever Christina wants to accomplish, she probably will!

Love Signs!

Of course, Christina's future also holds the promise of love and romance. She's a pure romantic at heart—something you probably figured out after you heard her croon those emotional ballads, like "I Turn to You" and "Blessed."

According to her love chart, Christina's perfect love matches are with guys born under the sign of Leo (like 'N Sync's J. C. Chasez), Aries (like *Buffy the Vampire Slayer*'s Nicholas Brendon), Libra (like 'N Sync's Chris Kirkpatrick), or Aquarius (like Backstreet Boy Nick Carter)—of course, that's not to say she'd totally reject Mr. Right if he didn't fall under one of those star signs. According to the stars, dudes who fall under these signs have the traits and qualities that would best complement Christina's—in other words, they'd definitely get along!

We looked through our star charts and came up with some mate traits that might make guys compatible with Sagittarian Christina. If Christina ever did pair up with someone who was born under one of these four signs, the relationship could be positively cosmic!

Here goes . . .

Lovely Leo

Sags and Leos could have loads in common, from their passion for music to their love of travel. Leos and Christina could definitely understand each other. Leos have the personality to light up a room, so those born under this sign could definitely appeal to Christina's sense of fun.

Awesome Aries

Many awesome Aries have the outgoing, magnetic personalities to get themselves noticed. A Sag like Christina might be attracted to an Aries's energy and enthusiasm for living. Maybe they could come up with plans to share the spotlight together, too.

Loving Libra

Wild, wacky, fun-loving, and always spontaneous, loving Libras tend to also be intelligent, fair, and very open-minded. A Libra can be the type of guy who feels protective toward a girl and would love to take care of someone special— qualities Christina could definitely appreciate. Libras also tend to be gentle, devoted and, most importantly, patient— that means a Libra guy would be able to withstand those long tour schedules that take Christina away from home for so long.

Dreamy Aquarius

Totally typical Aquarius guys tend to be goofy, silly, a little scatterbrained (sometimes!), unpredictable, and inventive. Guys born under the sign of the Water Bearer can be the type who always have their heads in the clouds, dreaming of the future. Christina's not afraid to think big either, so she and an Aquarius dude might get along swimmingly. Christina might enjoy an Aquarian's oddball antics and his silly sense of humor.

With so much talent, determination, and will to succeed, there's no doubt Christina Aguilera is a star who's destined to shine brightly for years to come.

The Future's
So Bright...

And where will that star be shining? Hmmm—could be music, movies, or TV!

Right now, of course, Christina is concentrating on making music and bringing it to her fans around the world. "I've been waiting for this moment all my life," Christina told *Teen People* magazine. "I want to focus on my singing, to make it the best it can be."

In 1999, in an effort to introduce her music to a new, wider range of fans, Christina played some concert dates with Lilith Fair, the concert series created by singer Sarah McLachlan that features only female singers. She stuck close to home, playing dates in Cincinnati, Ohio, and Pittsburgh, Pennsylvania. "For a bunch of women coming together, we thought it would be cool to show some real soul and roots," Christina told the *New York Daily News*. Those shows featured Christina on her own—without her usual group of dancers behind her. It marks a definite milestone for her, and she's totally thrilled to be a part of it.

Playing at Lilith Fair is just a part of Christina's grand plan—she wants to be regarded as a serious artist, one who's going to be around for a long, long time. "I've worked too hard to be known as just some come-and-go teen artist," she told the *New York Daily News*. "I want to be singing forever."

But although Christina is devoted to her singing career, she's also been dipping her toes into the acting waters as well. She's already filmed an appearance on *Beverly Hills, 90210*, the huge hit series on Fox-TV—she sang "Genie in a Bottle" and had a few speaking lines as well. She's also received offers from directors and producers of feature films. Right now, Christina's saying no to most of those offers—but might she make the jump sometime soon?

It makes sense that Christina might want to explore other outlets for her abundant talents. After all, fellow *MMCer* Britney Spears parlayed her mega-smash pop music career into TV appearances on *Dawson's Creek*—and it looks like Britney may even have a sitcom created just for her.

Christina also idolizes Whitney Houston, who's had quite the successful movie career herself. Like Whitney, Christina is expressive, lovely, and extraordinarily gifted—there's no reason she couldn't light up the movie screen the way she lights up a stage.

And singing and acting aren't the only things in Christina's future; she also recognizes the value of her education. She spent most of 1998 with a tutor, determined to graduate from high school, which she did, with flying colors. (She chose to continue studying with a tutor so she could fulfill her various work commitments.) Christina also plans to resume her formal education one day soon—she knows how important it is to build up her brainpower! "I think it's important to have a full education, so you're prepared, no matter what happens in your life," she told *Teen Beat* magazine. "There's so much I still want to do—so many things I want to accomplish in my life. I want to do it all!"

Of course, nothing is beyond

Lilith Fair

The Lilith Fair concert series was created in 1997 by singer-songwriter Sarah McLachlan. The idea behind it was simple—to celebrate the contributions of women singers and songwriters, the artists themselves needed to hit the road and tour together. Powerful, talented women such as Sheryl Crow, the Dixie Chicks, the Indigo Girls, Monica, and Sixpence None the Richer have joined forces to create one of the most successful concert series in history (creatively and financially— Lilith Fair has been second only to OzzFest as a concert money maker).

the reach of this young artist *Mademoiselle* magazine dubbed "One of the People to Watch in the New Millennium!" It's clear, Christina already has the power to make it all happen!

The Last Word!

Whatever Christina does choose to do with her life, there's no way she'll give up her music. She's spent so many years of her young life building her career and getting to the top of her form—there's just no way she's throw that away, ever. No matter what other opportunities come her way, Christina plans to remain true to her first love—singing. And with that golden girl voice, there's no doubt she'll always remain a great success at it. Christina herself, however, gets the last word about her future: "I don't know what I'd be doing if I didn't have singing and music in my life," she told *16* magazine. "I've been so blessed. I have everything I could possibly need in my life—wonderful friends, an amazing family and now this career. I know it will take a lot of work to stay on top in the music business—but I never minded hard work at all! And this has all been so worth it—every second of it has just been the best!"

Fan Section

HOW TO REACH CHRISTINA

Snail Mail

Christina Aguilera Fan Club
244 Madison Avenue
Suite 314
New York, NY 10016
or
c/o RCA Records
1540 Broadway
New York, NY 10036

Just like you, Christina loves getting mail—she loves flipping through your letters and hearing everything you have to say. She does try to get to as many letters as possible, but she admits it does take some time.

To increase your chances of a personal response from Christina, make your letter extra-special.

Always include a photo of yourself—it makes the letter more personal (and it gives Christina a face to go along with the words on the page). Also, if you include a self-addressed stamped envelope, you're more likely to receive a reply. And it wouldn't hurt to write your letter on funky stationery—maybe you could choose some bright, vibrant colors that really make your letter stand out.

Finally, don't stress out if you don't get a reply, like, tomorrow. Christina is working so very hard these days, and she often just doesn't get the time to sit down and concentrate on her fan mail—even though it's one of the most important things in the world to her. Don't be disappointed if it takes a while to receive an answer to your letter—and always remember that your letters really do make her smile.

46

E-Mail

Christinaaguilera@mailcity.com

Christina checks in with her E-mail as often as she can, and she tries to answer as many of your messages as possible. It's an excellent way to stay connected to Christina.

Christina on the Web!

The Internet is chock-full of sites and spots where you can get all the 411 about Christina as well as chat with other Christina devotees.

The official Christina Web sites are:

www.peeps.com/christina
www.Christina-A.com

To check out Christina Merchandise (like hats, T-shirts, etc.), plug into:

ChristinaA.howfun.com

There are a slew of alternative sites as well. (For easy access to more sites, you'll want to begin with a search engine like Yahoo, Alta Vista, or Lycos. Type in the name Christina Aguilera and you'll get a list of all the coolest sites.) Here are some of the best ones:

christinanet.virtualave.net
www.listen.to/christinaAguilera
www.fly.to/CAGalaxy
members.tripod.com/c_a_online/
come.to/christinacentral

Web Pages!

There are thousands and thousands of Christina Web pages out there on the Internet, almost all of them created by fans, for fans. These pages are a majorly cool way to reach out and chat with Web friends, as well to keep closely connected to Christina and what's going on with her. But be warned: These Web pages are unofficial, and often include information that is outdated, unsubstantiated, and sometimes completely untrue. Log on and download at your own risk, and definitely don't believe everything your read on the Web.

Christina Online!

Christina has done a number of chats with fans—most notably, she

47

Etta James

One of Christina's strongest musical influences is Etta James, who was a 1993 inductee into the Rock 'n' Roll Hall of Fame. Etta has been a presence in the jazz world for over four decades, blurring the lines between R&B, pop, gospel, and blues. Her gritty, emotional, and rich voice has been an inspiration to many singers,

who aspire to combine strong voices with lyrics that, at times, are almost painful to listen to—Etta really sings about life's sadness and disappointment.

chatted on Zoog Disney, and was a huge hit. You can always check out America Online for the latest, upcoming Christina events.

But be forewarned! Christina is not someone who goes into chat rooms on her own. Although she loves participating in chats with fans, it's always through a reputable company like America Online, and it's always in a formatted, scheduled arena. If you're chatting somewhere else and someone claims to be Christina Aguilera, don't believe it, 'cause it's simply not true.

Christina Facts at Your Fingertips

Full Name: Christina Maria Aguilera
Last Name Is Pronounced: A-ghee-lera
Birthday: December 18, 1980
Birthplace: Staten Island, New York
Hometown: Wexford, Pennsylvania
Ethnic heritage: 1/2 Irish-American; 1/2 Ecuadoran
Family: Parents are Shelley and Fausto; siblings are Casey (16), Stephanie and Rachael (13), and Michael (3)
Height: 5'7"
Hair: Very blond
Eyes: Blue
Life's Goals: "To be a successful recording artist, to move into acting without giving up singing (like Whitney Houston did!), to learn to speak Spanish and play piano, and to visit South America."

Favorites

Music: Whitney Houston, Etta James, Julie Andrews, Mariah Carey, B. B. King, and Etta James
Actors: Johnny Depp and Ben Affleck
Sports: Baseball and volleyball
Food: Tacos
Favorite Disney Movies: *Mulan* (of course!) and *The Little Mermaid*
Hobbies: Shopping, watching movies, and hanging out with good friends
Favorite Scary Movie: *Psycho*—the original!
Best Present She Ever Received: A Barbie kitchen—according to Christina, it was "da bomb!"

Zapping Those Christina Rumors!

It's amazing. As soon as someone gets a hit song, appears on a smash TV show or in a huge movie, or makes it major on MTV, you suddenly start hearing a whole bunch of rumors about them. Christina's no exception—even before "Genie in a Bottle" hit number one on the pop charts, the rumor mill was churning out stories about her. Here are just some of them—and the real truth you need to know!

Rumor:
Christina and Britney Spears hate each other.
Truth:
Not even! The pair have been close friends since their *MMC* days and remain buds to this day. "When Britney's album came out, I was the first to buy it," Christina says. "I've seen Web sites where fans are trying to pit one of us against the other. It's so ridiculous—taking sides is so ridiculous."

Rumor:
Christina is dating Justin Timberlake or Nick Carter or J. C. Chasez.
Truth:
Christina doesn't have a steady guy right now. While she knows a number of famous hotties, she doesn't date any of them either.

Rumor:
That's not really Christina singing. The producers in the studio created her sound.
Truth:
Whoa, is that ever a lame rumor! That's most definitely

Christina hitting those high notes—that powerful, magical voice is all hers. Although the producers work wonders to create amazing musical sounds, they're smart enough not to fool with a great vocalist like Christina.

Rumor:
Christina actually hates the song "Genie in a Bottle."
Truth:
Christina admits that when she first heard the song, she really wasn't crazy about it. "To tell the truth . . . I don't know if I should say this . . . but I didn't want to record 'Genie in a Bottle' as my first single," she told MTV. "Now of course, I have no regrets."

Rumor:
Christina is part Ecuadoran.
Truth:
Yes, she is, and she's very proud of that fact—she's hoping to do a Spanish language album in the future.

Rumor:
Christina is quitting singing to pursue acting.

B.B. King

Born Riley King, B.B. has long been considered one of the finest, purest blues singers and guitar players who ever lived. He started his career during the 1940s, playing gospel and blues music on

street corners in Memphis, Tennessee. He still performs more than three hundred concert dates yearly, to the delight of blues lovers across the country. One bit of B.B. trivia you must know—he named his guitar Lucille.

Truth:

Right now, Christina is concentrating completely on singing—her first love. But she definitely wouldn't rule out acting in the future.

Rumor:

Christina's into piercings and tattoos.

Truth:

Not unless her earlobes count! Christina's not into either of those trends, except that she does love wearing earrings in her ears!

Rumor:

Christina has major bad attitude—she's been known to totally dis her fans when they ask for her autograph.

Truth:

Not, not, not! Christina loves her fans, and always tries to be gracious when someone approaches her. She'd never go out of her way to hurt anyone's feelings. And as far as attitude goes, Christina has absolutely none—except, of course, for a positive one. She's thrilled about her success, and grateful for everything good that's happened in her life. No attitude here. "My mom would kill me if I ever got a big head," says Christina. "I'm thankful every day for the blessings in my life."

Rumor:

Christina has a crush on singer Enrique Iglesias.

Truth:

Yes, she does! She totally considers Enrique her fantasy dream man!

How to Look Like Christina!

When Christina was a thirteen-year-old member of the *Mickey Mouse Club*, she wore her dirty-blond hair long, loose, and flowing. She considered herself a bit of a tomboy, favoring jeans, overalls, and big shirts to dresses or anything fancy.

But these days, Christina totally enjoys dressing like a girl. She enjoys decking out in trendy clothes and she really does love shopping in all the coolest boutiques and shops. With a little imagination (and a whole lot of positive attitude) you can look like Christina too.

Hair

Christina wears her pale blond hair straight, brushed forward toward her face, but as her old *Mickey Mouse Club* photos show, she's actually got pretty wavy hair. To recreate Christina's cool coif, use your blow dryer and a monster round brush to smooth out your hair, then brush it forward to frame your face. As for the zigzag part Christina favors, just use a comb to maneuver the roots of your hair and create this awesome look.

For a night out, Christina might spend a little more time on her hair than usual, and she might add some styling gels or mousse to add volume and body. But for the most part, Christina really prefers muss-free, easy hairstyles that don't take a lot of time.

And to protect her hair from the harsh rays of the sun, Christina likes wearing baseball caps and hats—a habit everyone should get into, especially when the summer sun is really blazing down.

Makeup

When Christina is onstage performing or appearing on television, she has to wear an absolute ton of makeup. Maybe that's why when she's just hanging out, she likes to keep it simple. For your best daytime Christina look, you might want to follow her lead:

• Start with a matte foundation that perfectly matches your skin tone. Apply with a sponge to keep the foundation smooth and blended in, moving toward your jawline. When the foundation is totally blended into your skin, polish it off with a light matching powder—that will keep you from looking shiny.

• Brush a mauve or pale pink blush on the apples of your cheeks only (no one wants to have stripes on her face!).

• If you want to concentrate on your eyes and make them look really big, start by lining them with a simple dark brown, taupe, or gray pencil. Speckle the pencil along your lash line to avoid a sharp, harsh line. Follow with a brown-black mascara—one coat will keep the clumps away. (A neat trick that makeup artists use—clean off the mascara brush with a tissue before applying it. That will also keep the clumping under control.) Finally, use a brown, mauve, or pearly pink shadow—Christina favors natural colors. If your complexion is really fair, like Christina's, you definitely want to stay away from unnatural colors (blue, purple, or green shadow looks really fake)—stick to neutrals, like pale yellows and browns.

• If you want to make your lips stand out, like Christina's do, start with a lip pencil; stick to those in the rust or brownish-red family. Fill in with matte lipstick. For a natural everyday look, you might want to ditch the lipstick altogether and stick to gloss in a fun flavor.

• Always keep your look natural. Christina knows that less is more when it comes to daytime makeup, so never pile it on, and stay away from harsh colors. Fresh, clean, and natural is the way Christina likes to look for everyday.

Christina Loves the Nightlife!

Of course, when the sun goes down and the neon lights brighten up, Christina often adds some extra pizzazz to her makeup. She loves brushing on glimmery, sparkling glitter to her cheeks, her eyes, her neck, and even her shoulders. Nighttime is also the right time for brighter colors, and Christina definitely loves using hot lipstick colors like red or a frosted eye shadow for some added sparkle.

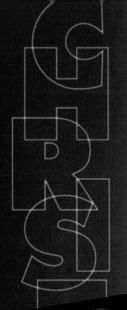

Clothes

Offstage, Christina is into comfy, trendy, casual, and cute outfits. She loves current fashions, but she never gets too way out. And she admits to having a major soft spot for super-feminine things. Basically, although she likes looking up-to-date and fashionable, she's really interested in comfort and style.

Christina definitely has a thing for cropped tops. She loves little sweaters and T-shirts that leave

her toned midriff bare. She also adores long, flowy skirts that almost graze the floor—she wears them so they fall just to her ankles. And of course, she's a jeans girl—she tops hers with little white cotton blouses edged in ruffles or ribbons, crocheted sweaters, or T-shirts in bright colors, like red or turquoise.

And when Christina is onstage, look out—she totally glams out in a big way. At a recent awards show, Christina took the stage in a sophisticated ensemble of gorgeous black floor-length skirt and a black shrug over a daring black tube top.

If You Want to Dress Like Christina . . .

. . . you don't have to spend a fortune. Check out vintage clothing stores for romantic, lacy tops and handmade sweaters.

. . . you can mix and match the tops and bottoms you buy at the mall. Team up a long skirt with a trendy little print sweater; invest in a pair of really dark blue jeans and top it with an extra-special, very girly white cotton blouse or a cropped short-sleeved sweater.

. . . be bold and try something totally differ- ent—buy some clothes in an outra- geous color, for example. Or if you usu- ally wear sweats and flannel shirts, try out some- thing amazing- ly old-fash- ioned. Christina is definitely not afraid to step out in a brand-new style.

Jewelry and Accessories

Christina's into jewelry big time—specifically, silver jewelry. You may have seen her sporting a gorgeous silver butterfly ring on the pointer finger of her right hand—that ring is one of her favorites, and it's rare that she isn't wearing it. She also adores bangle bracelets—silver, of course, but also colorful, beaded bracelets she wears stacked from her wrist

to just below her elbow.

Christina really loves butter- flies, and so, as you'd imagine, she's totally into butterfly clips and barrettes. She clips them into her hair, of course, but she also clips them onto her collars or onto the belt loops of her jeans. With a little imagination and creativity, you can probably think of a bunch of ways to use these adorable bar- rettes—they're an inexpensive and easy way to add major coolness to your clothes.

From Top to Toe

Christina never leaves the house without perfectly polished nails and toes. For her fingernails, Christina prefers keeping things clear and clean—as in French manicures (the kind when the tips of the nails are white and the base of the nail is natural) or the palest of nail colors. But for her toes, Christina goes completely wild—she loves vampy reds and rusts, and sometimes even uses blue or green!

Bonus Pop Quiz!

Could You and Christina Be Best Friends?

You're totally nuts over Christina's style of pop music. You think she's one of the coolest singers you've ever heard. And of course, you can't get enough of her smash debut album and her awesome, danceable videos.

But do you have what it takes to be part of Christina's crew—one of her closest, tightest true blues? Do you share tastes in music, movies and hobbies? What about values, ideals and ambitions? Well, there's only one way to find out—read this book, then take this little quiz and see if you've got what it takes to spend quality best-buddy time with Christina Aguilera.

1. You and Christina are going out for a day of shopping—what stores do you hit first?

(a) Trendy ones that sell the latest name-brand fashions
(b) Stores that sell preppy clothes that never go out of style
(c) Stores that sell sporty clothes for fun on and off the playing field

2. You're buying Christina some CDs for her birthday—which do you choose?

(a) Rap and hip-hop
(b) Albums by a great female vocalists—anyone from Mariah Carey to Julie Andrews
(c) Country

3. You and Christina are studying together—what subjects is she tutoring you in?

(a) History and economics
(b) Science and English
(c) Math and biology

4. You're spending a Saturday afternoon with Christina—what activities do you plan for the day?

(a) Something active, like a volleyball game at the beach—anything that gets you out in the fresh air and sunshine
(b) An afternoon playing video games at home
(c) You let Christina do all the planning and just go along with what she chooses

5. You want to be more like Christina—what attitude or motto do you try and adopt?

(a) Work hard and make your dreams come true!

(b) Live life to the fullest!

(c) Treat others as you'd like to be treated

6. What type of music does Christina feel spiritually and culturally tuned into?

(a) Country music—artists like Garth Brooks and the Dixie Chicks

(b) Alternative—artists like Nirvana and Pearl Jam

(c) The new Latin sound—artists like Ricky Martin and Jennifer Lopez

7. What's Christina's idea of a really scary movie?

(a) *Scream*

(b) *The Blair Witch Project*

(c) Alfred Hitchcock's original *Psycho*

8. Christina sometimes finds it tough being in the spotlight all the time—what could you do to make her feel better?

(a) Give her all your love and support, and let her know how much her friendship means to you

(b) Tell her how lucky she is to be in show business, and encourage her to get over her blue feelings

(c) Tell her what you'd give to trade places with her

9. When you and Christina get together, what do you most often chat about?

(a) All the famous people she's met and what she thinks of them

(b) Definitely clothes, movies, and guys, but also the hopes and dreams you only feel comfortable sharing with her

(c) Show business—you love asking her questions about it, and getting her advice on how you can be a part of it too

10. What do you do to show how much Christina means to you?

(a) You show her love and respect—you keep her secrets and support her in everything she does

(b) You make her laugh when she's feeling low and give her a shoulder to cry on when she's feeling down

(c) You let her know you're always there for her, and you treat her like the special person she is—and let her know you appreciate it when she treats you the same way

55

Answers

1. A
2. B
3. B
4. A
5. It's a trick question—all these sayings express feelings Christina believes in.
6. C
7. C
8. A
9. B
10. Another trick—all three are great ways to show Christina how much her friendship means to you.

How'd You Do?

10 matches: A serious bud-match—you and Christina would get along like sisters!

7-9 matches: Not too shabby—you know an awful lot about Christina, and the two of you would probably get along really well.

4-6 matches: Hmmm, looks like you and Christina don't share that much common ground.

0-3 matches: No way! Better read this book again, 'cause it doesn't take a genie to know you and Christina have nothing at all in common!

Fan Fun!
Create Your Own Personal Letter to Christina!
Tell Her How You Feel in a Clip-Out Letter!

You know Christina loves to hear from her fans. If you're one of them, have we got a cool feature for you!

We've created a way excellent form letter to Christina—you can either copy it on your own stationery, or fill in the blanks, clip the letter from this book or make a copy, and send it to her. The items we left blank are things we thought you might want to personalize—how many times you've listened to her CD, how many times you've watched her video on MTV, and exactly how much you love her.

After you're through writing your letter, you can mail it one of the addresses we gave you—you'll be sure your personal thoughts and best wishes for Christina will reach her.

Date: _____

Dear Christina,

I think you're a really great singer. I just bought your debut album and I think it's awesome. I listen to it _____ times a day. I especially love "Genie in a Bottle"—I think it's an amazing song. I listen to it while I _____ and it makes me want to dance. My best friends and I like to listen to your song while we _____ . I think you're such a _____ dresser. If I met you in person, I'd tell you all about _____. I admire you very much, and I think one day, I would like to pursue a career of my own in _____. I always try to catch your videos on MTV—you totally rock! I hope I get a chance to meet you when you come to do a concert in _____. I promise I'll be in the first row, with a sign that says, _____. I love you soooo much—I'll always be your #1 fan.

Love always,

_____

About the Author

JACKIE ROBB is a freelance writer who lives and works in the New York City area. She works for a variety of teen magazines, and is the author of *Britney Spears: The Unauthorized Biography*.

She is currently working on several other books on young artists and performers, a book on teen dating, a movie script, and a play. She lives with her husband, Arthur, and dedicates this and all her writing to him.